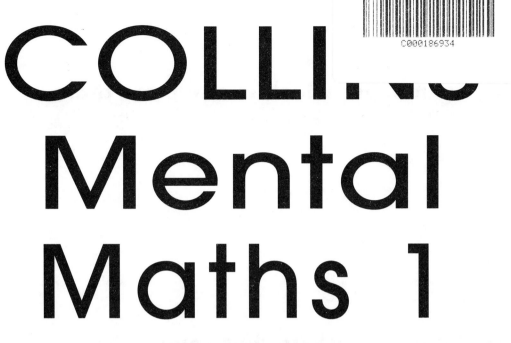

COLLINS
Mental
Maths 1

Jan Henley

Collins Educational

An imprint of HarperCollins*Publishers*

Counting on

Write the number which is one more than:

1. 4

2. 7

3. two

4. 0

5. five

Write the two numbers that come next.

6. 5, 6, 7, ☐, ☐

7. 0, 1, 2, 3, ☐, ☐

Use the number line to help.
Write the number you land on.

8. Start on 4 count on 3.

9. Start on 7 count on 2.

10. Start on 0 count on 6.

11. Count on from 3 to 7. How many did you count?

12. Count on from 8 to 10. How many did you count?

Counting back

Write the number which is one less than:

1. 4

2. nine

3. 7

4. 1

5. six

Write the two numbers that come next.

6. 5, 4, 3, ☐, ☐

7. 10, 9, 8, ☐, ☐

0 1 2 3 4 5 6 7 8 9 10

Use the number line to help.
Write the number you land on.

8. Start on 3 count back 1.

9. Start on 8 count back 2.

10. Start on 4 count back 3.

11. Count back from 8 to 3. How many did you count?

12. Count back from 5 to 0. How many did you count?

Number bonds to 5

1. 3 + 0 = ☐
2. 5 - 1 = ☐
3. 2 + 3 = ☐
4. 1 + 4 = ☐
5. 0 + 2 = ☐
6. 4 - 2 = ☐
7. 3 + 0 = ☐
8. 2 + 2 = ☐
9. 3 - 3 = ☐
10. 5 - 3 = ☐
11. 4 - 3 = ☐
12. 2 + 1 = ☐

Make these triangles add up to 5.

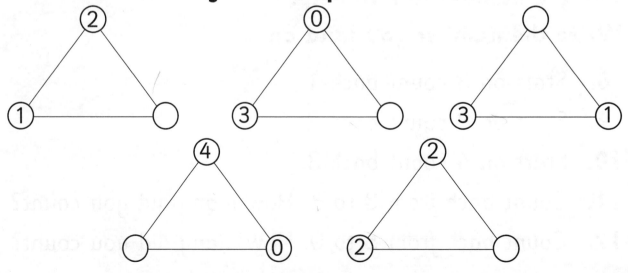

Number bonds to 10

1. 6 + 1 = ☐
2. 3 + 4 = ☐
3. 5 + 2 = ☐
4. 6 - 1 = ☐
5. 8 - 2 = ☐
6. 7 + 2 = ☐
7. 9 - 4 = ☐
8. 3 + 7 = ☐
9. 10 - 2 = ☐
10. 8 - 4 = ☐
11. 9 + 1 = ☐
12. 7 - 1 = ☐

Which coins could you add to make each purse add up to 10p? Draw the coins in your book.

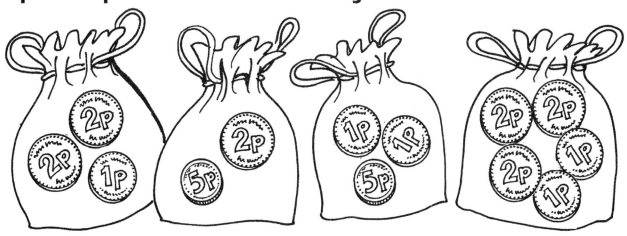

1. 4 + 1 = ☐

2. 7 - 2 = ☐

3. 1 more than 8

4. What comes next? 4, 5, 6, ☐

5. 1 less than 9

6. 3 + 4 = ☐

7. 8 - 2 = ☐

8. 7 - 0 = ☐

9. 1 more than 5

10. 1 less than 7

11. What comes next? 10, 9, 8, ☐

12. 7 + 3 = ☐

How much is in each purse?

Counting to 20

1. What is 1 more than 12?

2. What is 1 less than 11?

3. What is 1 less than 20?

4. What is 1 more than 15?

Fill in the missing numbers.

5. 12, ☐, 14, 15

6. 8, 9, 10, ☐

7. 17, 16, ☐, 14

8. 12, 11, ☐, 9

9. What is 2 more than 17?

10. What number is 2 less than 11?

11. What is 3 more than 9?

12. What is 3 less than 18?

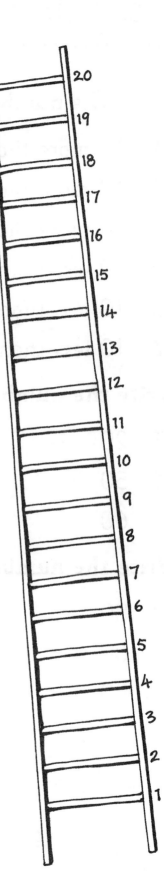

Counting in 10s

Write the number which is:

1. 10 more than 20
2. 10 more than 50
3. 10 more than 70
4. 10 less than 40
5. 10 less than 90
6. 10 less than 30

Write the number which is three tens more than:

7. 20
8. 50
9. 60

Write the number which is five tens less than:

10. 80
11. 60
12. 90

Counting in 2s

Write the next number.

1. 0, 2, 4, ☐

2. 8, 10, 12, ☐

3. 1, 3, 5, 7, ☐

4. 11, 13, 15, ☐

Write the missing numbers.

5. 3, 5, ☐, 9, 11

6. 6, 8, 10, ☐, 14

7. 13, ☐, 17, 19

8. 14, ☐, 18, 20

9. Write the number which is 2 less than 12.

10. What is 2 more than 18?

11. 12 is 2 more than 10. True or false?

12. 11 is 2 less than 9. True or false?

More number bonds to 10

1. $8 + \square = 9$
2. $7 - \square = 3$
3. $\square + 3 = 9$
4. $\square - 2 = 6$
5. $4 + \square = 7$
6. $6 - \square = 4$
7. $9 - \square = 3$
8. $\square + \square = 10$
9. $\square + 5 = 7$
10. $\square - \square = 5$
11. $\square - 4 = 3$
12. $\square - \square = 7$

Make each square add up to 10.

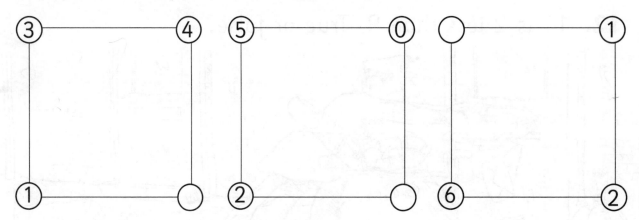

Doubles and halves

1. 2 + 2 = ☐
2. Double 3
3. Half of 8
4. 10 = ☐ + ☐
5. Double 1
6. 4 + 4 = ☐
7. 2 = ☐ + ☐
8. Half of 6
9. 0 + 0 = ☐
10. Double 5
11. Half of 2
12. 3 + 3 = ☐

Copy and complete these sentences.

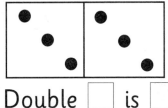

Double ☐ is ☐

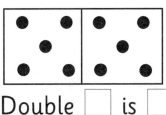

Double ☐ is ☐

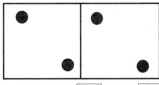

Double ☐ is ☐

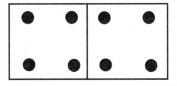

Double ☐ is ☐

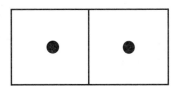

Double ☐ is ☐

CHECK UP 2

1. $8 + \boxed{} = 10$

2. 2 more than 7

3. Double 4

4. $7 + 2 = \boxed{}$

5. $9 - 5 = \boxed{}$

6. 2 less than 8

7. 1 more than 19

8. Half of 4

9. 3, 5, 7, $\boxed{}$. What comes next?

10. 2 more than 11

11. $6 + \boxed{} = 9$

12. $\boxed{} - 3 = 6$

Write down the missing numbers.

12

Starting with 10

1. $10 + 4 = \square$

2. $10 - 4 = \square$

3. $10 - \square = 7$

4. $10 - \square = 8$

5. $10p + 6p = \square$

6. $10 - 0 = \square$

7. $10 + 0 = \square$

8. $10 - 5 = \square$

9. $10 + 9 = \square$

10. $10p + \square = 12p$

11. $10 - \square = 2$

12. $10 - 6 = \square$

Shopping

What change would I get from 10p if I bought:

1.   **2.**   **3.**   **4.**

Starting with 20

1. $20 + 5 = \boxed{}$

2. $20p + 8p = \boxed{}$

3. $20 - 6 = \boxed{}$

4. $20 - 9 = \boxed{}$

5. $20 + \boxed{} = 23$

6. $20 + \boxed{} = 29$

7. $20 - \boxed{} = 17$

8. $20 - \boxed{} = 12$

9. $20 + 4 = \boxed{}$

10. $20 - 7 = \boxed{}$

11. $20 - \boxed{} = 16$

12. $20 + 0 = \boxed{}$

Shopping

What change would I get from 20p if I bought:

1. an apple?

2. a banana?

3. an orange?

4. a pear?

5. an apple and an orange?

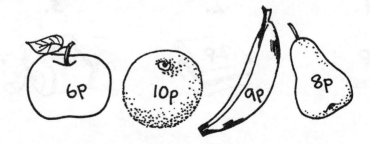

Adding and subtracting 'teens' numbers

1. $16 + 3 = \boxed{}$
2. $15 + \boxed{} = 19$
3. $17 + 1 = \boxed{}$
4. $\boxed{} + 5 = 18$
5. $19 - 2 = \boxed{}$
6. $17 - 5 = \boxed{}$
7. $\boxed{} - 3 = 13$
8. $15 - \boxed{} = 12$
9. $14 - 11 = \boxed{}$
10. $\boxed{} - 5 = 14$
11. $14 + 4 = \boxed{}$
12. $\boxed{} + 5 = 18$

How old?

Luke (15)

Anna (13)

Rajiv (16)

1. Sam is 2 years older than Luke.
2. Tina is 4 years younger than Rajiv.
3. Sunil is 5 years older than Anna.
4. Ben is 4 years younger than Luke.

CHECK UP 3

1. 17 + 2 = ☐

2. 10 more than 40

3. 10p + 6p = ☐

4. 20 - 5 = ☐

5. What comes next? 90, 80, 70, ☐

6. 20 + ☐ = 29

7. 15 - ☐ = 12

8. 10 - ☐ = 4

9. 3 tens less than 40

10. 20p - ☐ p = 12p

11. ☐ - 6 = 12

12. ☐ + 7 = 27

Totals

Use these numbers 7 10 5 3 **to complete these sums:**

1. ☐ + ☐ = 10

2. ☐ + ☐ = 12

3. ☐ + ☐ = 8

4. ☐ + ☐ = 17

Crossing 10

Try doing these in two steps like this:

$6 + 7 = 6 + 4 + 3 = 10 + 3 = 13$

HELP BOX

1. $8 + 4 = \square$
2. $7 + 5 = \square$
3. $9 + \square = 12$
4. $6 + \square = 11$
5. $9p + 5p = \square$
6. $8 + \square = 14$
7. $7 + 6 = \square$
8. $8 + 7 = \square$
9. $\square + \square = 17$
10. $\square + 5p = 13p$
11. $\square + 9 = 16$
12. $\square + \square = 15$

Complete the missing numbers.

1. $9 + 4 = 9 + 1 + \square = 10 + \square = 13$
2. $7 + 5 = 7 + \square + 2 = 10 + 2 = \square$
3. $8 + 4 = \square + 2 + 2 = \square + 2 = 12$
4. $6 + 8 = 6 + \square + 4 = 10 + \square = \square$

More doubles and halves

1. Double 6
2. Half of 14
3. Two fives
4. How many legs on two dogs?
5. Half of 20
6. Half of 16
7. Double 9
8. How many fingers on 2 hands?
9. How many days in 2 weeks?
10. Half of 10
11. Double 8
12. Half of 12

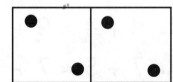

Playing cards

Copy and complete.

1.

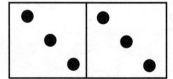

Double ☐ is ☐

2.

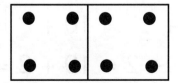

Double ☐ is ☐

3.

Double ☐ is ☐

Near doubles

HELP BOX

6 + 5 is the same as double 5 then add on 1, or double 6 then subtract 1. Now try these.

1. $7 + 6 =$ ☐
2. $8 + 9 =$ ☐
3. $5 + 6 =$ ☐
4. $8 + 7 =$ ☐
5. $4 + 5 =$ ☐
6. $10 + 9 =$ ☐

Adding 9

HELP BOX

A quick way to add 9 is to add 10 then subtract 1. Now try these.

1. $3 + 9 =$ ☐
2. $5 + 9 =$ ☐
3. $8 + 9 =$ ☐
4. $6 + 9 =$ ☐
5. $4 + 9 =$ ☐
6. $9 + 9 =$ ☐

1. Two 8s

2. 9 plus 6

3. $7 + \square = 14$

4. $6p + 5p = \square$

5. $6 + 7 = \square$

6. Half of 12

7. $8 + \square = 15$

8. $\square + 5 = 12$

9. Double 9

10. $\square + \square = 17$

11. $7p + 7p = \square$

12. $\square + \square = 13$

Making 20

Complete all of these questions so that the answer is 20.

1. $16 + \square = 20$

2. $13 + \square = 20$

3. $7 + \square = 20$

4. $11 + \square = 20$

Large and small

Write down the larger number.

1. 7p, 5p

2. 15, 18

3. 11, 1

Write down the smaller number.

4. 12, 2

5. 8p, 18p

6. 10, 9

Write down the smallest number.

7. 3, 1, 6

8. 10, 8, 12

9. 7, 17, 0

Write down the largest number.

10. 15, 8, 3

11. 19, 20, 9

12. 11, 1, 12

In between

Write any number that comes between each pair
of numbers so that all three numbers are in order.

1. 2 ☐ 7
2. 5 ☐ 10
3. 7 ☐ 12
4. 6 ☐ 11
5. 3 ☐ 5

6. 10 ☐ 15
7. 13 ☐ 19
8. 18 ☐ 20
9. 20 ☐ 30
10. 19 ☐ 24

True or false?

1. 31 is between 29 and 32
2. 17 is between 18 and 20
3. 25 is between 20 and 30
4. 14 is between 11 and 13
5. 19 is between 18 and 22

Ordering numbers

Write these numbers in order starting with the smallest.

  1. 9, 7, 6, 8

  2. 8, 2, 9, 4

  3. 16, 5, 10, 18

Write these numbers in order starting with the largest.

  4. 2, 0, 5, 3, 7

  5. 15, 20, 17, 21

  6. 3, 9, 12, 10

Write a number between:

  7. 2 and 5

  8. 10 and 15

  9. 17 and 19

Write all the numbers between:

  10. 23 and 28

  11. 9 and 12

  12. 13 and 20

Ordinal numbers

Look at these letters of the alphabet.
Which letter is:

1. first?

2. 5th?

3. tenth?

4. 8th?

5. third?

6. 12th?

7. 4th?

8. 2nd?

9. 11th?

10. sixth?

11. 9th?

12. seventh?

CHECK UP 5

1. Write a number between 5 and 8.

2. Which is larger, 9 or 19?

3. The 🐱 is 1st. True or false?

4. The 🐰 is 3rd. True or false?

5. The 🐭 is 5th. True or false?

Put these in order, the largest first.

6. 14, 8, 12, 16, 9

7. 17, 22, 19, 24

8. Write a number between 9 and 15.

9. 12 comes between 13 and 15. True or false?

10. Which is more, 15p or 5p?

Put these in order, the smallest first.

11. 14, 10, 4, 24

12. 30p, 20p, 23p, 10p

Adding 3 numbers

1. $3 + 2 + 4 =$ ☐
2. $5 + 3 + 2 =$ ☐
3. $4p + 3p + 5p =$ ☐
4. $6 + 2 + 3 =$ ☐
5. $4 + ☐ + 2 = 8$
6. $☐ + 5 + 3 = 12$
7. $6p + 5p + ☐ = 12p$
8. $1 + ☐ + 6 = 9$
9. $☐ + ☐ + 2 = 13$
10. $☐ + ☐ + ☐ = 10$
11. $1 + ☐ + ☐ = 12$
12. $5 + ☐ + 4 = 11$

Triangles

Make these triangles add up to the numbers inside.

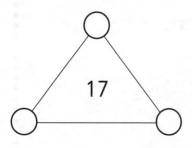

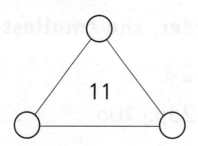

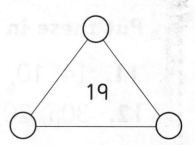

Take 3 numbers

Write sums to make these totals.

1. 8 = ☐ + ☐

2. 5 = ☐ + ☐

3. 7 = ☐ + ☐

4. 10 = ☐ + ☐ + ☐

Write addition sums to make these totals
using only 1, 2, 5 and 6.

5. 9

6. 13

7. 12

8. 8

Use the numbers 4, 6, 7 and 9 to write addition
sums for these totals.

9. 17

10. 16

11. 20

12. 19

What is...?

What number is:

1. 10 more than 6?
2. 1 more than 19?
3. 10 less than 17?
4. one before 43?
5. 2 more than 18?
6. 1 less than 50?
7. 2 less than 15?
8. 10 more than 2?
9. 10 less than 70?
10. 2 more than 20?
11. 2 less than 5?
12. one before 10?

True or false?

1. 21 is 10 more than 31
2. 15 is 2 more than 12
3. 47 is 1 more than 48
4. 15 is 10 more than 25
5. 36 is 1 more than 37

What comes next?

Write the next number.

1. 3, 6, 9, 12, ☐
2. 4, 6, 8, ☐
3. 5, 10, 15, ☐
4. 10, 20, 30, ☐
5. 80, 70, 60, ☐
6. 11, 13, 15, 17, ☐

7. 22, 24, 26, ☐
8. 20, 18, 16, 14, ☐
9. 25, 30, 35,
10. 9, 7, 5, ☐
11. 5, 8, 11, 14, ☐
12. 25, 20, 15, ☐

Number hops

Write the missing numbers.

1.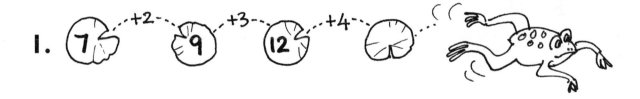

2.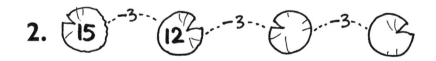

3.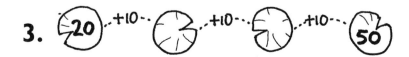

CHECK UP 6

1. $8 + 5 + 2 = \square$

2. $\square + 3 + 7 = 16$

What comes next?

3. 15, 20, 25, $\square$

4. 12, 9, 6, $\square$

5. 8, 6, 4, 2, $\square$

Use these numbers 7, 4, 5. Show addition sums to make:

6. 11

7. 9

8. 16

9. What is 1 more than 39?

10. What is 2 less than 30?

11. $9p + 4p + \square = 18p$

12. $\square + \square + \square = 16$

How much?

Write the total amount in each purse.

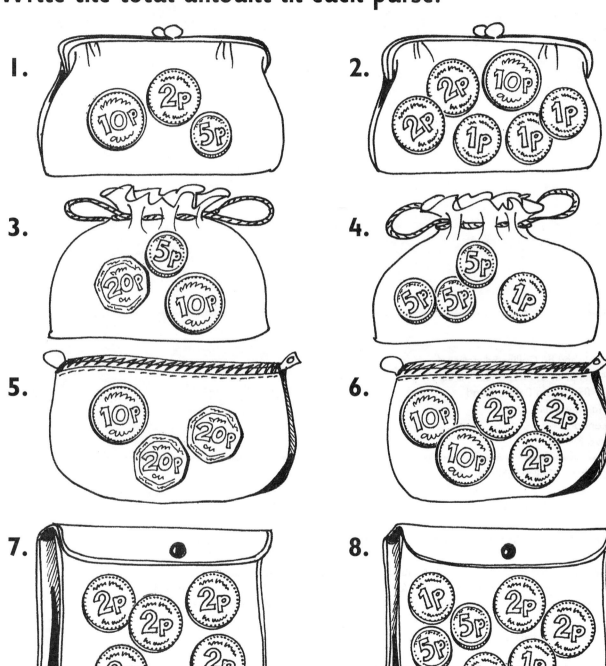

Published by Collins Educational
An imprint of HarperCollins*Publishers*
77-85 Fulham Palace Road
Hammersmith
London
W6 8JB

© HarperCollinsPublishers 1998

ISBN 000 315 381 9

Author: Jan Henley

Illustrations: Jean de Lemos, Martin Remphry

Design: Sylvia Kwan

Printed by Martin's the Printers, Berwick on Tweed